I have not stopped giving thanks for you,
remembering you in my prayers.

EPHESIANS 1:16

For you, my sister,

_____

with love,

_____

date

_____

Thank heaven for those who have always known us ...
We belong to each other and always shall.

SARAH ORNE JEWETT

The BEST SISTER in the WORLD

HOWARD BOOKS

A DIVISION OF SIMON & SCHUSTER

New York · London · Toronto · Sydney

Our purpose at Howard Books is to:

- *Increase faith* in the hearts of growing Christians
- *Inspire holiness* in the lives of believers
- *Instill hope* in the hearts of struggling people everywhere

Because He's coming again!

HOWARD
BOOKS

Published by Howard Books, a division of Simon & Schuster, Inc.
1230 Avenue of the Americas, New York, NY 10020
www.howardpublishing.com

The Best Sister in the World © 2007 by Dave Bordon & Associates, LLC

Library of Congress Cataloging-in-Publication Data

The best sister in the world / [edited by Chrys Howard].
        p. cm.
    Includes bibliographical references.
    ISBN-13: 978-1-4165-4173-8
    ISBN-10:   1-4165-4173-X
    ISBN-13: 978-1-58229-693-7 (gift ed.)
    ISBN-10:   1-58229-693-6 (gift ed.)
    1. Family—Religious aspects—Christianity. 2. Sisters—Family relationships. 3. Sisters—Religious life. I. Howard, Chrys, 1953–
    BT707.7.B475 2007
    242'.643—dc22

                                          2007015584

10 9 8 7 6 5 4 3 2 1

HOWARD and colophon are registered trademarks of Simon & Schuster, Inc.

Manufactured in the United States of America

For information regarding special discounts for bulk purchases, please contact: Simon & Schuster Special Sales at 1-800-456-6798 or business@simonandschuster.com.

Project developed by Bordon Books, Tulsa, Oklahoma
Project writing and compilation by Shawna McMurry and Christy Phillippe in association with Bordon Books
Edited by Chrys Howard
Cover design by Lori Jackson, LJ Design

CONTENTS

WHAT IS A SISTER?

She's someone you can't live without—but sometimes you'd really like to!

She's someone who knows you through and through but sometimes you wish she didn't!

She's also someone who'll stick up for you like a mother hen.

And she'll give you the shirt off her back.

Yes—sometimes she's a bother but you know you'd never trade her for anyone else in the world.

Because . . . she's your one-of-a-kind Sister!

R. NORTON

INTRODUCTION

Having a sister is one of life's greatest blessings. Sisters share a unique bond that makes them the best at understanding, encouraging, and strengthening one another. They've learned, through their shared memories, how to make each other laugh, when to give a comforting hug, and the art of loving each other unconditionally.

The Best Sister in the World celebrates the joy of sisters everywhere, but most especially, it honors you, the unique and special sister in my own heart. I hope this book inspires, encourages, and shows my appreciation to you, my sister. I'm so honored and thankful that God has placed you in my life.

Sis, you're the best!

You're the

BEST

SISTER

in the World Because...

You Understand

Me.

Your sister is a reflection of your own life,
upbringing, and circumstances.
When you look at her, you see your past,
present, and future.

CASSANDRA M. HARRINGTON

> Whoever does the will of my Father in heaven
> is my brother and sister.
>
> MATTHEW 12:50

Siblings tend to have a unique understanding of one another, born out of similar experiences and backgrounds. Because they have shared the same childhood and parents, they know better than even the closest of friends where the other is coming from.

This level of understanding among siblings is what makes Jesus' reference to Christians as His brothers and sisters so significant. When Jesus came to earth in the form of a man, He didn't come as the king everyone was expecting. He would never have been able to relate to us. No, Jesus came to earth as we did, a baby, and then was raised by common parents. He experienced what it's like to be a child, to have siblings, to work for a living. Because of His experiences, He understands us in much the same way that siblings understand one another.

How complete God's love for us truly is, that He would include the special bond between siblings in His relationship with us.

A LETTER TO MY SISTER

Dear Sis,

You have known me since the day I was born. You helped change my diapers and take care of me when I was a baby. You played with me when I was bored. You taught me all the new things you learned at school and filled me in on the latest fashions. The first time a boy broke my heart, you understood my pain and were there for me with a shoulder to cry on. Now that we're grown, you're the first person I call when I need to talk to someone. I can depend on you to truly understand the workings of my heart.

Thank you, Sis, for being such a blessing to me. You have enriched my life in so many ways all along my journey, and I can't imagine life without you.

Love,

Your Sister

In thee my soul

shall own

combined the sister

and the friend.

CATHERINE KILLIGREW

We talk alike,

We look alike,

We think alike.

We are as one—yet we are not.

We are unique,

We are different.

We are individuals—we are sisters!

PRISCILLA COTTON

WHY I'M THANKFUL YOU'RE MY SISTER . . .

. . . Between the two of us,
someone is sure to remember
Mom's birthday!

The noblest pleasure is
the joy of understanding.

LEONARDO DA VINCI

SISTERS, SISTERS

By Paula Miller

Whenever I see that old favorite, *White Christmas,* I wait for the song that has brought both tears and a smile to my face, "Sisters." Sparkling blue dresses and enormous feathered fans sweep the Haynes Sisters into an elegant dining room to sing.

Having an identical twin sister seems quite intriguing to some. I've often been asked, "What's it like having a twin?" My response is, "What's it like not having a twin?" While most people wonder what it was like to share a room, friends, a car, and an apartment, I can never figure out how someone could have grown up without a best friend by their side at all times.

Sometimes she knew me better than I knew myself.

We shared everything. From our love of chocolate and sappy romantic movies to the little gray and red Horizon that found its way into the ditch on more than one occasion. And clothes. We shared a closet full of clothes through elementary school and right on up until we had to divvy them up when I got married.

The funny part is now, ten years later, when we visit each

other, we both come down to the breakfast table wearing the same shirt. We live such a distance apart that we don't get the chance to shop together, but our tastes are still the same.

I still have to laugh over one holiday when we arrived at our parents' home wearing similar purple shirts. Even our "new" haircuts were the same. My husband approached my sister from behind and . . . well, suffice it to say, he thought it was me!

I recall one instance when my mom made us sit in different rooms and write a list of ten reasons we should be allowed to go somewhere. She still laughs when she tells us how eight out of the ten answers, right on down the list, were exactly the same and in the same order.

Now we live a good 100+ miles from each other, but it's rare indeed when the phone isn't ringing at one of our houses every morning of the week. More than likely we answer saying, "I was just about to call you."

Not much has ever come between my sister and me. Oh, we

had our share of arguments back in high school and college when we struggled between being twins and being our own person. But as anyone knows, fighting with a best friend never lasts long, and we usually hadn't quite finished our argument before one of us had already apologized.

So here's to twins, sisters, best friends. God has given us a special gift in each one.[1]

The capacity to care is the thing which gives life its deepest significance.

PABLO CASALS

✻ ✻ ✻ ✻ ✻

Heavenly Father,

It's nice to be understood, to know that someone else has traveled the same roads I have and seen the world from the same point of view. I have that relationship with my sister. She often knows what I'm thinking even before I say a word, and I feel as if I can talk to her about anything.

Thank You for my sister and for the many ways she is a blessing to me and my family. May she feel the same comfort she gives me of being truly understood and appreciated. When she needs someone to talk to, I hope she'll always know she can confide in me, but more importantly, I pray that she'll desire to confide in You, her heavenly Father.

Thank You for being that Friend and Confidante who knows us and loves us even more than a sibling is capable of and who understands our every thought and emotion.

Amen.

I THANK GOD for you,

my UNDERSTANDING sister!

You're the

BEST

SISTER

in the World Because...

We Know Each

Other's Secrets.

Secrets are things we give to others

to keep for us.

ELBERT HUBBARD

O LORD, you have searched me and you know me.
You know when I sit and when I rise;
you perceive my thoughts from afar.

PSALM 139:1–2

It's nice to have someone who knows everything about you, someone you can tell your deepest secrets to and know you'll never be judged for them. Sisters fill this role for each other.

There is someone else who knows all of your secrets, each detail about what makes you unique—your Heavenly Father. God's limitless knowledge of us can seem intimidating at times, especially if we think of Him as a harsh judge whose purpose may be to deal out judgment for our secret thoughts and actions. But this view of God doesn't fit His description in the Bible.

First John 4:16 states very simply: "God is love." His acute attention to each detail of our lives is motivated by His great love. So if you're ever tempted with feelings of insignificance, think about the vast time, love, and attention the Creator of the universe puts into knowing you.

A LETTER TO MY SISTER

Dear Sister,

You have always been the greatest at keeping a secret. When we were young, we shared a room, and we'd often stay up on the weekends talking late into the night. Sometimes we'd build a tent with our sheets and blankets, a secret club-house of sorts where the most sacred of confidences could be safely shared. We'd talk about things that seem silly now but were quite serious to us at the time—like my plan to dye my hair red or your secret stash of candy. We'd talk about the boys we admired and our dreams for the future.

Today, there are times when I call you to tell you about something that's been on my heart, and I can feel the warm cocoon of our secret clubhouse surrounding me all these years later.

Thank you, Sis, for being my closest friend and confidante.

Love,

Your Sister

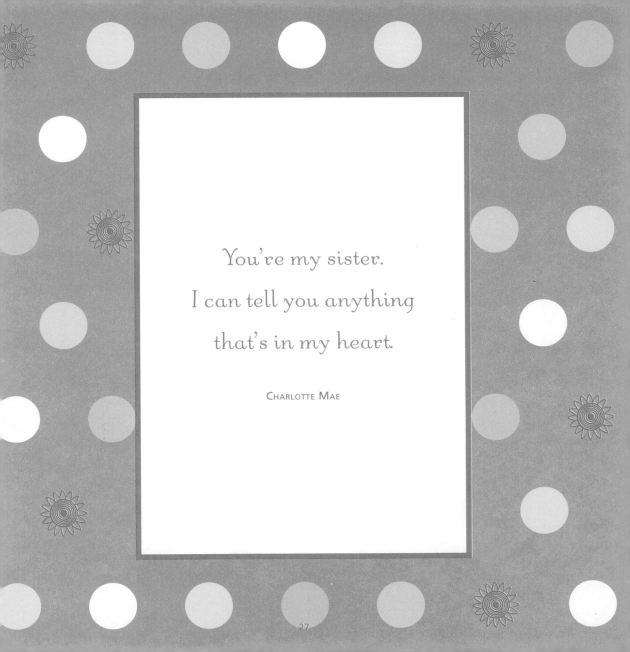

You're my sister.
I can tell you anything
that's in my heart.

CHARLOTTE MAE

27

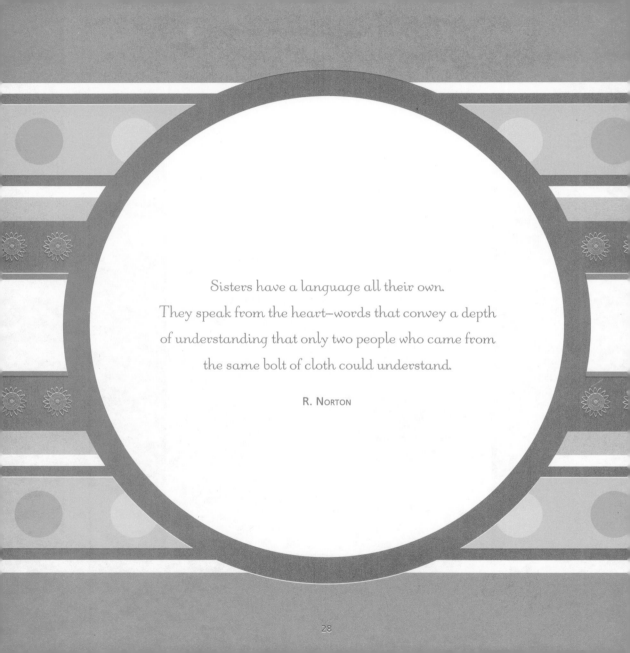

Sisters have a language all their own.
They speak from the heart—words that convey a depth
of understanding that only two people who came from
the same bolt of cloth could understand.

R. NORTON

SUNDAE CONFESSIONS:
BREAKING THE ICE-CREAM RULE

By Andrea D'Asaro

As the hottest days of the year approach, my thoughts turn to ice cream.

My mother, a zealous nutritionist, held all refined sugars in the category of unmitigated evil. When I was a child, she would call the hostess before I arrived at friends' birthday parties. "My daughter isn't allowed any cake or candy," she would warn sternly. I would sit alone at the end of the table while the other girls gobbled their goopy treats. When the hostess offered me an apple, I tried to look happy and avoid unwanted sympathy. I didn't want to cry.

My mother's goal was to raise pure, untainted children. Avoiding sugar—and the resulting flab and tooth decay—was more important than life itself. She would prophesy with morbid glee: "When you're lying in your grave, you won't have a single cavity in your mouth!"

For my sister, Lisa, and me, breaking the rules was the superglue that held us together. When we weren't fighting for scraps of parental attention, we were scheming to sneak candy and ice cream.

On Halloween, our mother allowed us to harvest trick-or-treat candy if we handed over all the contraband upon arriving home. Always practical, she would give it back out to the goblins and astronauts who came to our door. One year, Lisa and I contrived to hide half our hoard under our beds. At night, we gorged ourselves on Reese's Peanut Butter Cups and miniature Snickers bars.

Although we are both happily married, Lisa and I still take great joy in breaking the rules and indulging in the depravity of ice-cream sundaes. On a summer visit to our parents' house, we decide to sneak away to Friendly's. At the counter, with the sinful delight of the deceitful, Lisa and I contemplate our sundaes.

"I'm considering hot butterscotch and fudge with Swiss almond crunch and butterscotch ice cream," I tell Lisa. She is lost in thought, staring up at the selection of ice creams. I suspect she is trying to decide between chocolate chip mint ice cream with hot fudge, or vanilla with caramel sauce and chocolate jimmies.

The waiter, a bored high school student, brings the glossy sundae menus. The bright scoops slathered with sauces reel before my eyes. "Are you ready to order?" he asks. He is looking toward the entrance, perhaps expecting his girlfriend. He could care less about our high moment. He is tall and thin with brown hair falling over his pimply forehead.

"Let me ask a few questions," I say in a feigned voice of calm. "Does this sundae have two scoops or three?" I hold back an urge to order the super-duper five-scooper. My mouth is watering, my hands are cold, my speech is high-pitched and wavering.

The waiter slowly gets into the spirit of the thing as I press him with questions about the temperature of the hot fudge and the saltiness of nuts in the Swiss almond fudge. Lisa wants to know if the mint ice cream is very minty or mildly minty. Our taste buds are whipped into frenzy.

The waiter leans over us jotting notes on his pad. He carefully explains the types of sauces and options for whipped cream, leaving to check on supplies in the kitchen. After finalizing our orders, he asks: "How about if I just go wild on these sundaes?" We agree.

We fidget until our sundaes finally arrive: pure bliss. With my long spoon, I plunge through the frilly whipped cream and the hot sauce covering the frozen scoops nestled below. It's sweet, cold, hot, all at once. We trade tastes, making sure we scoop equal amounts of ice cream and sauce on each spoon. We gorge ourselves until our spoons clink on the bottom of the thick glass dishes. I see the waiter looking over at us. We sigh, contented.[2]

The memories we've shared since childhood,
the laughs we have enjoyed throughout the years, and the
secrets we have entrusted to each other—these are the things
that remind me that there is no one like you, sis.

VICTORIA CRANK

✺ ✺ ✺ ✺ ✺

Heavenly Father,

Sometimes it seems as if my sister knows me better than anyone in the world. She's known my secrets since we were little. We've shared many of the same experiences and even know certain things about each other without ever having to say a word.

As well as my sister knows me, You know me even better. You know my hidden thoughts and my secret ambitions. You know of strengths in me that others never see, and You see all my weaknesses that I try so hard to hide. There is nowhere I can go to hide from You. Yet, knowing everything there is to know about me, You love me and consider me Your precious child. You know and love me completely.

When I'm sorrowful, You are intimately acquainted with my grief. When I'm happy, Your joy over me knows no bounds. Thank You, Father, for the security found in being known and loved so well.

Amen.

I THANK GOD for you,

my sister, my CONFIDANTE!

You're the

BEST

SISTER

in the World Because...

We Have So Much
Fun Together.

Giggling under the covers
after Mother tells us
lights out. Laughing in
the movie theater at
the silly movie.
Snickering when the cute
boy walked by our table.
Laughing till we cried
when we bought the same
dress without knowing it.
All moments of sheer joy
shared by no one other
than you, my sister!

EMMA MARIE CLOUD

A cheerful heart is good medicine.

PROVERBS 17:22

No one can bring a ray of sunshine to an otherwise dismal situation quite like a sister. As much as you may try to resist her attempts to make you smile, she'll soon break down your defenses and have you laughing and feeling hopeful once again.

What a blessing that God gave us sisters to lift us up and help put smiles on our faces. In today's world, it is so easy to feel overwhelmed and unhappy. We also have a tendency to worry, which even further strips the joy from our lives. It's comforting to know that when we are down, our sisters will be there to cheer us on!

And we all need joy. Proverbs 17:22 has it right—laughter is good medicine. Its benefits are scientifically proven; it takes the edge off all the rough things we go through in life. And somehow, sisters just seem to know when to crack a joke or tickle us when we least expect it.

Thank God for sisters!

A LETTER TO MY SISTER

Dear Sis,

Whether I'm struggling to keep up with my flight on the wings of success or groveling in the depths of despair, you always seem to know just the thing to say or do to bring a smile to my face. Soon that smile turns to laughter, and my tension that once seemed so permanent quickly fades away.

I remember one night when I was feeling particularly overwhelmed. I'd talked to you briefly that day and thought I'd effectively disguised the tension building within me. That is, until you showed up on my doorstep with a half gallon of ice cream, two spoons, and an armful of romantic comedies. You forced me away from my piles of unfinished paperwork, and we spent the rest of the evening on my couch, laughing, sharing, and reminiscing over old times. My paperwork didn't get finished that night, but it did lose its power to intimidate me, and I woke up the next morning refreshed and ready to tackle the days ahead.

Thank you, Sister, for your ability to capture and pass along all the joys of life.

Love,

Your Sister

My sister can still make
me laugh and giggle
like a kid with the
funny faces she makes
and her crazy antics.
She is a riot to be with
and can brighten up
any day of mine by just
being herself.

DORIS VALENTINE

Having fun is one of the things
that sisters do best!

EMMA CHANTELLE

OF YELLOW-HAIRED DOLLS AND UGLY CLAY BOWLS

BY GAIL E. STROCK

A few months before my wedding, my mother and I were breezing through all the details that go along with planning a large wedding. My fiancé, on the other hand, was happily making our honeymoon arrangements. Dennis and I saw each other only on weekends, and we were looking forward to our two-week wedding trip.

About three weeks before our wedding, my parents moved into their newly built log home, where I shared a room with my younger sister. I spent what weeknights I could rooting through the boxes we'd moved from the old farmhouse, deciding what was my sister's and what I should move to our new apartment. Twenty-three years of nostalgia awaited me each evening. I opened box after box filled with high school yearbooks, 4-H ribbons, kites made from construction paper, paper plate seed-shakers, and crayon drawings. And at the bottom of one box, I'd discovered a homely brown clay bowl that only a child could have fashioned and only a mother could have loved. I couldn't remember making the bowl, so I assumed it was my sister's.

When my sister entered the room, I held up the lumpy clump and confidently announced, "Here, Sharon, this is yours." She grimaced and denied ever seeing the clay vagrant. But I was sure it was hers. So after she left the room, I slipped it under her pillow, a subtle way of saying, *This really is yours!*

She grinned the next morning at the practical joke, and I headed off to work—only to find the bowl in my purse at lunch. That night, I put it in her high school backpack where I hoped she would be forced to pull it out in front of all her friends. We spent the last week trying to outwit each other until last-minute wedding details took my attention.

A few days before the wedding, my sister approached me, towing a child's doll along by the foot. The doll stood about two feet high and had straw-yellow hair. I'd never seen it before. She simply said, "Here, Gail, this is yours." I told her it didn't belong to me, and even if it did, I'd have no use for it now and certainly wouldn't care to hand it down to a daughter if and when that time came. In other words, she could keep it. She walked away, and I completely missed seeing the mischievous twinkle in her eyes.

Our wedding day dawned bright and beautifully warm for early April. The church was full, my sister stood beside me as a bridesmaid, and we danced our hearts out at the reception. As the last few guests said their good-byes, I went from table to table with my mother gathering the fresh flowers for her and me. Dennis and I stopped back at my parents' home, changed clothes, loaded the car, and gave hugs and good-byes all around.

Our three-hour drive to the Poconos gave us a chance to relax and wallow in the pleasure of finally escaping together. We pulled into the resort, signed the register, found our cottage, and unloaded the car. I hauled my suitcase up onto the heart-shaped bed and flipped open the lid as my new husband came up behind me. He slipped his arms around my waist and then froze. There, inside my suitcase, atop all the clothing, was a yellow-haired doll looking up at me with outstretched arms. My husband's face turned to utter horror as he thought I'd brought my baby doll along with me on our honeymoon. I laughed so hard that it took a few minutes before I could explain that my little sister really got me good this time.[3]

Joy is the echo of God's life within us.

JOSEPH MARMION

* * * * *

Lord,

Even though we know each other inside out and I've heard all of her corny jokes more than once, my sister has a way about her that brings laughter to my heart whenever I'm around her. There's something electric about her personality that sparks excitement and joy about the simplest, everyday things. She knows, like no one else, how to turn my stress or grumpiness into laughter and joy. I used to envy this carefree quality in her personality, but now I'm so grateful for it.

Thank You, Father, for my wonderful sister. You made us with very different personalities, but as we grow, I'm learning how well we complement each other, and I'm seeing Your divine wisdom in our relationship. You've known all along how much we would need each other and how much happiness we would be able to add to one another's lives.

Bless my sister with joy-filled days. May she be a blessing to all those around her, just as she is to me.

Amen.

I THANK GOD for you,

my FUN-LOVING sister!

You're the

BEST

SISTER

in the World Because…

You Bring Out the

Best in Me.

A sister believes in you when you have

stopped believing in yourself—

she helps to bring out the potential in you

that she always knew existed.

F. NEWTON

As iron sharpens iron, so one man sharpens another.

PROVERBS 27:17

Sisters have a unique talent for nudging one another in the right direction. They can be straightforward with each other because they know they'll always be sisters, even if they disagree once in a while. Your sister can get away with giving constructive criticism that just wouldn't be received in the same way from a friend. The ability to do this stems from the love you share. Because of that love, you want the best for one another even if it means pointing out a flaw or giving a seemingly unwelcome word of advice.

In the same way, God's love manifests itself sometimes in direction and reproof for our lives. Although we sometimes find it difficult to receive and obey His instructions, He wants us to realize that they will ultimately lead us to a life of blessings. He always has our best interests at heart.

And sisters are the same. They love us and want our best even if they have to nudge us once in a while!

A TRIBUTE TO MY SISTER

No matter what, my sister, Yolanda, will always tell me the truth! That is one thing I love about her.

Since I'm very social, I often worry about my relationships with others and tend to lose it if I think someone's mad at me. So many times I've called her, pouring out my fears that I haven't pleased someone on my list. What is her response? She immediately tells me that I do not need to please others—God is the only One I should strive to please. Her words of truth have often brought me back to reality.

Then there are the many times she's encouraged me to say no when I'm stressed and overcommitted. Her voice of reason plays softly upon the strings of my mind, and I realize that she's right—I need to take care of myself rather than volunteering for everything.

I am so grateful that not only does she have a listening ear, but she tells me what I need to hear. She challenges me to be the best I can be. She's a great sister!

R. NORTON

A sister is someone

with whom you can dare

to be yourself.

LACEE BROWN

A true sister helps us think our best thoughts,

do our noblest deeds, be our finest selves.

AUTHOR UNKNOWN

MY SISTER, MYSELF

BY SALLY FRIEDMAN

I watch her as she crosses a busy street, step jaunty, head bent against a strong wind. I make a mental note to remind my sister that she really should cross streets more carefully in this traffic-choked town.

But as soon as we hug and sit down to talk, she'll dismiss that suggestion and move right on to the "agenda" she has: A list of the important subjects we must cover this afternoon when we've both managed to stop the world for a sister coffee date. Talks about crossing streets can wait.

Ruthie is not just my big sister; she is my alter ego, my confidante, my mirror, my opposite, my counterpoint. I cannot imagine life without her—and she's been around from the instant I was born two years after she was, destined to forever disrupt her status as an adored only child.

She's long since forgiven me for so altering her life, although my mother tells stories of the tortures she, my dispossessed elder, inflicted on me, the usurper. And I surely remember the fierce fights we had as teenagers, living in bedrooms next to one another when one of the oft-heard sounds was the banging of a door. "Stay out of here!" we would order one another furiously. Ten minutes later, we were giggling again.

As sisters, we never heeded Shakespeare's admonition of "Never a borrower or a lender be." What we had was community property. Every now and then, I'll still find something of Ruthie's—a scarf, a bracelet, a book—in a drawer or closet. It always reminds me that small pieces of our lives are in residence at one another's homes, and the idea pleases me.

Everyone says we're so different. And in so many ways we are.

Ruthie is rational, analytical and altogether sensible. Her emotions don't rule her head. Small but mighty, she is also disciplined enough to eat a perfectly balanced diet—and to faithfully attend her aerobics classes and do her strength training.

I live in my nerve endings, eye the treadmill that leers at me, and hang my jackets on it. My aerobics career lasted one week.

My sister is the family scholar, the sibling who read and read and read some more while I, the gadfly, partied. I wanted more of her academic diligence and determination. She wanted more of my social skills.

In midlife, we've borrowed from one another's stashes of strength, and we've happily shifted roles often and enthusiastically.

These days, my sister gives the best parties; I go to them—and then often stand in a corner marveling at my sister's ability to host disparate people effortlessly.

Now I'm the passionate member of a book group, and no matter how urgently I try to get Ruthie to join one, she hasn't. She's too busy having fun. . . .

Is something wrong with this picture?

We don't think so.

My sister and I have finally managed the feat that some unfortunate siblings never master: We've accepted one another as we are, and we've cast aside the labels that we thought might be glued to us forever.

It wasn't easy. It didn't happen overnight.

And believe me, there are still plenty of times when we drive each other crazy because, yes, we *are* different.

But Ruthie is the person who would walk barefoot across burning coals to help me. I'd do the same for her.

She is part of me, part of my journey through life, and the one person in the world with whom I shared both past and parents. We have our own language, a shorthand that I couldn't possibly explain to anyone else, and that often begins with the words, "Remember when?"

It's probably no coincidence that we "different" sisters have both ended up in the same career, that we are both writers who prefer the freelance life to a standard nine-to-fiver. It's also probably no coincidence that we share many of the same friends and most of the same values. And while we do not always share beliefs about politics and the state of the world, we do have remarkably similar laughs, voices and, yes, feet. We are blessed (or cursed) with high arches.

It doesn't matter to me that Ruthie, long divorced, fiercely independent, is far more unconventional than I am.

It doesn't matter to her that when we part from our precious coffee afternoons, I rush home to cook dinner while she dashes off to intriguing ethnic restaurants with her assortment of amazing friends.

What we share transcends those trifling differences.

Ruthie and I may squabble. We may even argue fiercely about the biggies, including the way to approach the challenges of our aging mother. But even if our styles, our habits, and our basic personalities are astonishingly different—the ying and yang of siblinghood—we are joined at the soul.

Yes, sisterhood is powerful. And complicated. And rich.

And nobody knows that better than a woman who's lucky enough to be a sister.[4]

A sister will love you for who you are, and yet inspire you to be what you could be.

CAROLINE B. GEORGE

＊　＊　＊　＊　＊

Heavenly Father,

My sister has always been my biggest fan, and I've been hers. She was at my basketball games, pom-poms in hand, ready to cheer for her big sister before she knew the difference between a basket and a foul. And I was always as proud as could be to watch her flutter across the stage gracefully in her dance recitals.

Now that we're grown, some of our activities have changed, but we're still there, as we always were, to cheer each other on. When I need a word of encouragement, I know I can always count on my sister to give me the boost of confidence I need. When she sees that I'm not living up to my potential, she gently reminds me of Your purpose for my life and nudges me in that direction once again.

Thank You for displaying Your endless love for me through my sister. You've strengthened me many times through her caring words and actions. With You and my sister in my corner, I know I can accomplish great things.

Amen.

I THANK GOD for you,

my INSPIRING sister!

You're the

BEST
SISTER
in the World Because...

You've Seen All My
Faults—and
Love Me Anyway.

Accept me as I am.

Only then will we discover each other.

FEDERICO FELLINI

[Love] always protects, always trusts, always hopes, always perseveres. Love never fails.

1 CORINTHIANS 13:7–8

In all your days spent with your sister as you grew up, you probably had your share of not-so-virtuous moments—moments when your need to have things your way superceded your sister's feelings or instances when you allowed your sister to take the blame for something you had done. Yet, no matter what the offense, there is probably nothing you could have done to make your sister turn her back on you—nothing that a sincere apology couldn't remedy.

If your sister, who is human and has the same types of flaws inherent in all of us, can love and forgive you in such a way, how much more accepting and forgiving must be the perfect love of God.

So as you approach His throne of grace, pour out your heart as you would to your sister. Feel the power of His acceptance by viewing yourself as His precious child who can do nothing to lessen His love.

A LETTER TO MY SISTER

Dear Sister,

You know all about me—the good, the bad, and the ugly. You were there when I threw fits to get my way as a child. You knew about the mischief I got into that our parents never found out about. You've seen me when I didn't have anyone to impress—and when I tried way too hard to impress others. Yet through it all, I've never doubted for a moment that you love me—sometimes in spite of my faults; many times because of them.

Thank you for being my loving sister. Thank you for being so patient with me and forgiving me when I need it. May you feel the same love and acceptance from me that you give me so willingly.

Love,

Your Sis

When you love people,
you do see their
faults—you just choose
to ignore them.

MILDRED APPLEBAUM

We love those who know the worst of us

and don't turn their faces away.

WALKER PERCY

MY PERFECT SISTER

By Carol Sterner

I grew up with the perfect sister. She was my senior by three-and-a-half years so maybe she made all her mistakes before I was old enough to remember them—but I have no recollection of her doing things like I did that got me into trouble.

I had no desire to be a troublemaker, but somehow I still managed to mess up. Like the time I very meticulously printed my second-grade teacher's name on the envelope for a valentine I planned to give her the next day—the words *Miss Williams* were deeply ingrained in the beautiful finish of the piano bench for posterity.

Another time, I energetically did a somersault across the bed. The heel of my shoe left an indentation in the wall, a permanent reminder of my lively exercise that is still there to this day.

Even more disastrous was the time I stepped on a loose board in our unfinished attic floor and suddenly fell through, my right leg protruding through the dining-room ceiling. There I dangled, until Mom came in and found me. With insulation and plaster strewn from wall to wall, that room could have been declared a disaster area.

My sister and I shared a bedroom with one double bed. She gave me many reminders of "my side" as opposed to "her side" by drawing an imaginary line down the center of the bed. Of course, most of the time it was very confining to be against the wall on "my side." But during the summer months, when it still was very warm at bedtime, I clung tenaciously to "my side" when we reversed our positions to sleep at the foot of the bed. My head was next to the breezy open window, and no amount of coaxing would make me give up "my side" then!

The windows of our bedroom were adorned with floor-length lacy white curtains. I loved the view of our backyard, and one day when I was watching the birds and squirrels out the window, I leaned a little too heavily on the lace curtain. Oops! A big hole in the fabric was the result. Mom had just recently washed, starched, and "stretched" those curtains—a tedious job of placing them on a frame with nails about one inch apart on all sides of the curtain—until they were dry. Needless to say, Mom was not happy when she saw what I had done.

When she asked who tore the hole, I couldn't bring myself

to tell the truth—and of course, my sister also said she didn't do it. The result was that the dreaded yardstick was administered to the backsides of both my sister and me—something we both remember to this day.

Despite all of my mistakes—and the fact that I got her into trouble on more than one occasion—my sister still forgives and loves me to this day, a reminder of the amazing unconditional love God has for us all.[5]

We forgive so long as we love.

FRANCOIS LA ROUCHEFOUCAULD

✳ ✳ ✳ ✳ ✳

Heavenly Father,

More than even my sister, You know all my faults—each unkind thought or selfish action—yet Your love for me never wavers. No matter what I do, You always see the best in me, the potential You've placed in me, rather than focusing on my weaknesses. In fact, You even choose to work through my weaknesses at times, bringing good out of them.

Thank You, Father, for Your unconditional love toward me and for a sister who is, for me, a tangible example of that love. By loving me even when I'm wrong, she shows me how limitless the boundaries of love can be. She helps me to understand how a love like Yours is even possible and to believe that it is meant for me.

I am grateful, Lord, for Your boundless love and for a sister who displays its power so naturally to me. Bless her today for her loving heart and forgiving spirit.

Amen.

I THANK GOD for you,

my FORGIVING sister!

You're the
BEST
SISTER
in the World Because...

We've Shared
Everything—Except
Boyfriends!

There is no delight in owning

anything unshared.

SENECA

Do not forget to do good and to share with others,
for with such sacrifices God is pleased.

HEBREWS 13:16

One of the great blessings of sisterhood is learning the joy of sharing. From sweaters and skirts to french fries and muffins to laughter and tears, sisters share everything with one another. Most of the time, this sharing happens willingly, sometimes under compulsion; yet one seldom hears of sisters looking back with regret at the things they shared with each other.

What seemed like an overcrowded bedroom becomes the cozy haven where precious memories were made. Even matters that were sources of conflict in childhood become springboards for laughter and reminiscing later on, spurring conversations such as, "Remember the time you snuck out of the house with my favorite outfit under your coat? Well, I guess it was worth it since you met the love of your life that night!"

What a great thing to learn—the art and power of sharing. And it's a great gift from God that we could learn it from our sisters!

Sisterhood is another word for sharing.

Whether it be sweaters or bracelets

or words—you know it's ok.

You may say it's not, but deep down,

you wouldn't have it any other way.

F. NEWTON

WHY I'M THANKFUL YOU'RE MY SISTER . . .

. . . You supply me with a nice
second wardrobe!

A TRIBUTE TO MY SISTERS BY HEART

As an only child, I was accustomed to having my own space, my own things, and a certain amount of privacy. However, when I moved into a dorm room with three other girls—all of whom had siblings and mostly sisters—I quickly learned that some of my ideas about privacy were to quickly become a thing of the past.

My new roommates had no qualms about congregating in my tiny bedroom uninvited and rummaging through my closet. Before I knew it, my sweaters, belts, and shoes were whisked away to other rooms to see how they would go with jeans and skirts from another closet. It took me a little while, but before long, I was timidly asking to go through their closets too. Soon, everything was community property, and when a special event came up, we made the rounds from room to room in search of the perfect outfit.

Several years after graduation, I was going through my closet and came across a belt and immediately thought of my roommate who had worn it more than I ever had. The next time I saw her, I told her it was all hers, and we had a good laugh over old times.

Thank You, Father, for these sisters by heart, who openly welcomed me into their lives and closets. They helped me to loosen up and gave me a taste of the joys of sisterhood.

SHAWNA MCMURRY

We share a kindred

spirit that comes

from being

sisters of the heart.

AUTHOR UNKNOWN

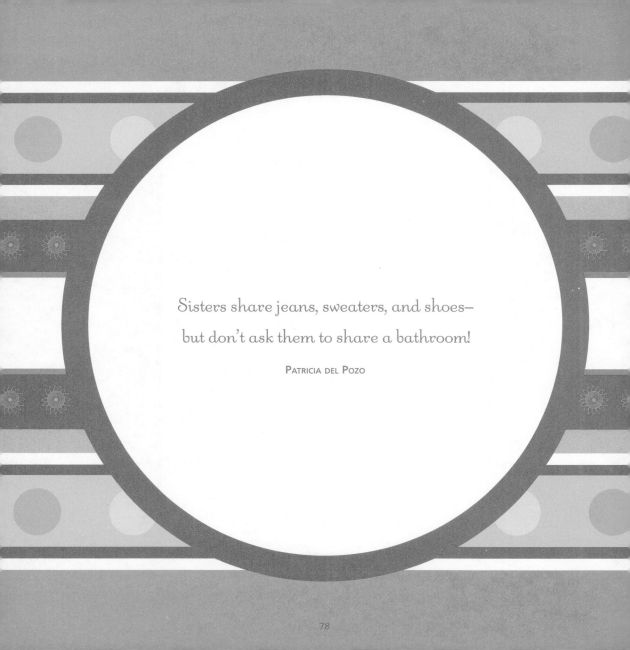

Sisters share jeans, sweaters, and shoes—
but don't ask them to share a bathroom!

PATRICIA DEL POZO

SISTER TWISTER

By Carol McAdoo Rehme

"Can I borrow your turquoise earrings?" my younger sister yelled from her bedroom across the hall. "The ones you got in Albuquerque?"

I teased the hair on the crown of my head, hoping to add some height. "No way. They're mine and today *I'm* going to wear them." I frowned at the reflection in my dresser mirror. "Besides, you never returned my mohair sweater."

"Oh, that. It's hanging on the hook in my school locker. At least, I *think* it is."

"And what about my tennis racket?" I demanded.

"Oh, probably still in my gym locker," Wanda appeared in the doorway of my room. "Anyway, back to the earrings . . ."

"But you lose everything of mine!"

"I don't," she said.

"You do." I glared.

"I don't either." She glared back.

"You do, too!" Hands on my hips, I stared her down. "There's not a single hair clip left in my jewelry box, you still haven't found my daisy raincoat, and just where are my bangle bracelets?" My boots tapped an irritated staccato as I crossed the room to grab my schoolbag.

"Well . . . I . . . I . . . I did return your red gloves." Wanda lowered her head to avoid my scowl.

"One. You returned one glove. What am I supposed to do with only one red glove anyway?"

She jerked to attention with a sly smile. "One? Why, you could always use it to wave at Bradley Gilmore," she simpered. "Maybe *then* he would finally notice you."

I gasped. She knew about my crush on Bradley? I hadn't told *anyone,* not even my diary. How could she? I whirled to face her and met her cheeky grin.

"Honestly, even my secrets aren't safe from you. You steal those, too!" I tried to frown, but her giggles were contagious and soon my own joined hers.

"Now," she said, "about those turquoise earrings . . ."

"Absolutely not." I shook my head firmly, then suggested, "Why don't you wear the silver hoops I loaned you last week? They'll look cute."

"Cool," she smiled sweetly. "And, uh, by the way—could you spare a minute to help me look for them?"[6]

*Sisters teach us that in all things it is
better to give than to receive.*

AUTHOR UNKNOWN

✸ ✸ ✸ ✸ ✸

Lord,

Thank You for the many lessons You taught me through my sister. Among the most valuable concepts I learned from her are the joy of sharing and the futility of holding on too tightly to material possessions.

When we were younger, we had many a disagreement about "mine" and "yours." Oh, the anger I felt when my sister spilled nail polish on my favorite shirt! But through the years, we learned to give up our claims to things and found that we were much happier when we willingly shared with each other.

Now that we're grown, some of my fondest memories are of evenings spent rummaging through each other's closets or of being able to make my sister's face light up by loaning her my favorite shoes.

I often think about my sister when I'm compelled to share something I have with a neighbor or friend, and I'm grateful to her for introducing me to this great joy of life.

Amen.

I THANK GOD for you,

my SHARING sister!

You're the
BEST
SISTER
in the World Because...

You Always Know

Just the Right

Thing to Say.

There can be no situation in life in which

the conversation of my dear sister

will not administer some comfort to me.

LADY MARY WORTLEY MONTAGU

A man finds joy in giving an apt reply—
and how good is a timely word!

PROVERBS 15:23

We all learn from an early age that the phrase "words can never hurt me" just isn't true. Words can be powerful weapons that can be hurtful to even the toughest personalities. By the same token, the "right" words, spoken at the right moment, are like perfect diamonds chosen for a wedding ring. They glisten and bring joy to the receiver.

Who better to speak these "right" words to us when we need it than our sisters. Because of the unique relationship they have with us, they are more aware of what we personally need to hear in a time of crisis. And with God's leading, they can become a tool of great encouragement.

And what is the best source for these "encouraging words?" The Bible. It is full of appropriate messages of love, comfort, and inspiration. God knows the power of a good word and He is overjoyed when He sees sisters communicating good words to one other.

A LETTER TO MY SISTER

Dear Sis,

I'm not sure how you do it, but you always seem to know just what to say to make me feel better when I'm down. Maybe it's because you've known me all my life. You can tell when I need to laugh and when a good cry is more in order; and you know just the words to say to immediately produce either reaction.

Because of our history together, I often don't even have to speak for you to know what's on my heart. You can sometimes put my feelings into words better than I ever could, and I can always depend on you to be there for me with a listening ear when I need to talk.

Thank you, Sister, for being such an encouragement to me. Thank you for having such insight into my heart and being sensitive to my needs.

Love,

Your Sister

When I am
falling apart,
I know that my sister
will always put me
back together.

EMMA CHANTELLE

Sisters are for sharing laughter at happy times—and putting on a pot of tea when troubles arise.

LACEE BROWN

WHY I'M THANKFUL YOU'RE MY SISTER...

...I can call you
at four in the morning,
and it won't matter.

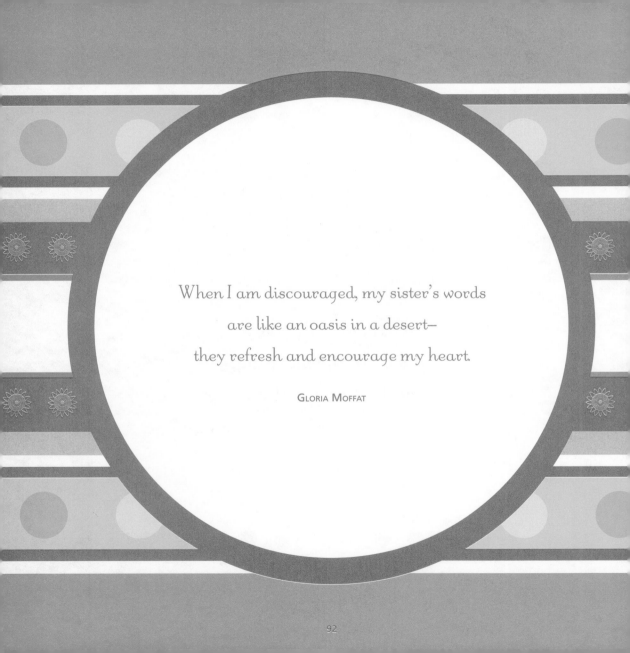

When I am discouraged, my sister's words
are like an oasis in a desert—
they refresh and encourage my heart.

GLORIA MOFFAT

THE MIRACLE OF MY SISTER'S LAUGHING

By Deborah Hedstrom-Page

Some of the lowest days of my life came shortly after my husband's death. While still grieving, I came face-to-face with the reality of raising our four children alone. The funeral was over, friends and family gone. It was the kids and me, each of us grieving as our ages and personalities allowed. One son angry, the other quiet; one daughter demanding, the other mothering. And somehow I was supposed to deal with it all. I was supposed to give the sole direction, the lone understanding, and single wise responses.

While at the bottom of this inadequacy well, my sister arrived. She'd planned it that way, saving her visit until everyone else had left. Within hours, the closeness we had shared in the past came flooding back. She let me talk and cry but also helped me begin doing things. We got my kids returned to school and then started tackling projects. We started with my closet since its half emptiness constantly reminded me of my now gone husband. We decided to install a closet organizer, so I could add my sweaters and other clothes to fill it up.

Things didn't go well. While she held up one end, I'd try to install and hammer the other. Nothing fit. As we improvised, things got worse. Then in the midst of our frustration, I noticed the picture on the organizer's box. A two-dimensional woman smiled back from it while she single-handedly installed what my sister and I were failing to do. While still holding up my end, I said, "Hey, Jeanne, look at that picture. I wish!"

She took one look at the woman and said, "Yeah, right. She's even wearing a dress." That's when it happened. Somehow the whole situation turned into a joke.

Every fumble we made, every board that slipped, every screw that refused to twist brought us back to the perfect lady on the box and made us laugh. We laughed until the tears came. We laughed until we had to drop the organizer and run for the bathroom.

It was the first time I'd laughed in weeks.

That laughter happened years ago, yet I remember it as if it happened yesterday. It changed nothing, yet it changed everything. My kids were still grieving. I was still hurting, overwhelmed, and inadequate. But when I hugged my sister good-bye, I knew God had used her to give me a miracle. For in the hard months following her departure, on my worst days, I inevitably opened my closet and spotted my slightly tilting organizer. No matter how I felt, I just couldn't help smiling.[7]

*Sisters enjoy a special freedom—
the freedom to share their deepest thoughts and feelings;
the freedom to be themselves.*

PHILLIP E. WAINWRIGHT

❋ ❋ ❋ ❋ ❋

Heavenly Father,

Thank You for the intimate bond I share with my sister. The closeness between us enables us to understand one another to a degree not found in other friendships. It gives us the ability to encourage and strengthen each other and to build each other up as we both pursue Your will for our lives.

Please help me to take full advantage of any opportunity I'm given to be a source of strength and encouragement for my sister. Make me sensitive to her needs and the detailed workings of her heart. May I never get too busy with my own affairs to take time out for my sister when she needs me.

I'm so grateful for my sister, for the special relationship between us, and for the time we're able to spend together. Please bless her and her loved ones today.

Amen.

I THANK GOD for you,

my THOUGHTFUL sister!

You're the

BEST
SISTER

in the World Because...

You've Been with
Me Through Good
Times and Bad.

A ministering angel

shall my sister be.

WILLIAM SHAKESPEARE

Rejoice with those who rejoice;
mourn with those who mourn.

ROMANS 12:15

It may come quite naturally for you to empathize with your sister. Because you're so familiar with the rhythms of her heart, her sadness makes your heart sad, and her joy easily becomes your joy as well. This unique ability to see things through each other's eyes has likely been a great source of comfort and encouragement to you both on many occasions.

In the New Testament, fellow Christians are referred to repeatedly as our "brothers and sisters in Christ." Does this mean it's possible for us to empathize with other Christians, who are not physically related to us, on the same level we do with our natural siblings? The Bible indicates that it is possible and even desirable. God wants us to grow so close to one another as His dear children that we are able to feel one another's pain and take joy in each other's victories.

A LETTER TO MY SISTER

Dear Sis,

When I took the stage in my first school play, you were there cheering me on. When I fell off my bike and skinned my knee, you were by my side, helping me home to the comfort of Mom and a bandage. You stuck by me when a bully at school convinced all my friends to avoid me.

You've been with me during the birth of each of my children, holding my hand through the pain and rejoicing with me over a new life. The time, love, and attention you pour into each of your nieces' and nephews' lives have made such a difference in our family.

Thank you, Sister, for being so loving and for sticking by my side through thick and thin. May you feel today how valuable and treasured you are to me and to my family and know of the special place you hold in each of our hearts.

Love,

Your Sister

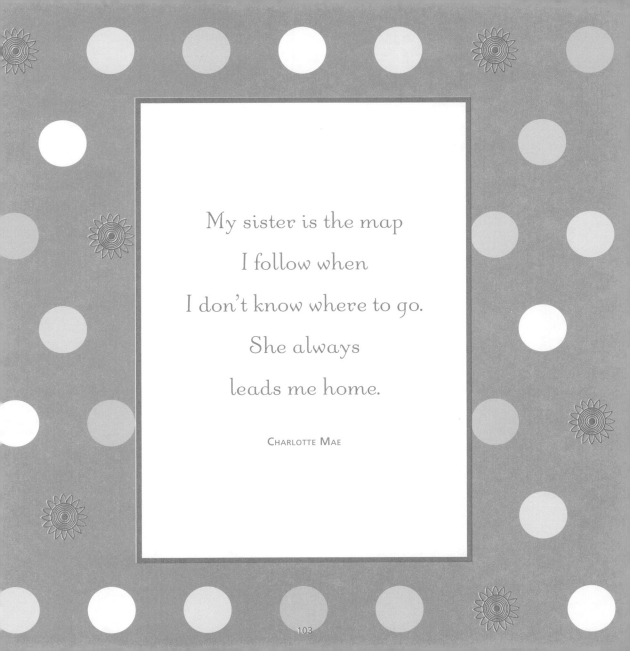

My sister is the map

I follow when

I don't know where to go.

She always

leads me home.

CHARLOTTE MAE

My sister is always there for me—

she is like an angel—

she helps me through my bad hair days.

EMMA B. CLOUD

SPIT PROMISES

BY DAWN BRAULICK

With five years difference in our ages, people still said how uncanny it was for us to look so much alike. My sister and I shared a lot of the same facial features and, of course, we both have long, red hair. Well, at least I had hair until I started chemotherapy. My long red locks fell from my head in clumps as the treatments went on.

I touched my now-bald head. Fresh tears sprang to my eyes. People would not say we looked alike now. My sister, Marlanea, was flying in from Montana to see me. She didn't know how bad I was going to look. I wanted to prepare her for the shock or protect her from what she was going to see. I had always watched over her, trying to keep her safe and out of harm's way. She was born on my fifth birthday. Our mother said she was my birthday present. I took that seriously, and I loved her with all my heart.

We went through our growing-up years inseparable. We were each other's best companion. Our parents used to tell us that we should have been twins for how much we resembled each other, for how close we were.

We even thought alike. When we were shopping, we would buy each other small gifts—from T-shirts to coffee mugs—but most of the time we bought each other the same thing. We shared a connection that was beyond most people's understanding.

Now adults, we live in different states. She called me on the phone, and all I said was "Hello." Instantly, she said, "I know something is wrong. Tell me. What is it?"

No longer amazed at her uncanny ability to tell when something is wrong, I told her that at eight o'clock that morning I had to put our family pet to sleep. Together in silence, we cried. Tears I could not shed earlier that morning now flowed freely as I talked on the phone with my sister.

Since finding out that I have cancer, she has called almost daily, concern always in her voice, but cheerful nonetheless. She has sent me a funny card every week, a bright ray of hope that makes me believe life will be okay again.

During one tearful phone conversation, she told me she knew for sure that I would not die from this intruder called cancer.

"Oh, how do you know?" I asked through my tears.

"Because when we were really small, we made a spit promise that we could only die if the other sister was ready to die, too. And I'm not ready to die yet, so neither can you."

We never discussed what would happen if we broke a spit promise. But we both knew that it had to be serious.

I heard her cab pull up in front of my house. My sister, my friend, had arrived.

With trembling hands, I reached up and touched my bald head once more before I opened the door to my best friend—my sister.

There she was, the sun shining behind her, lighting her up like the angel I had always thought her to be. There she was in her tight jeans and a T-shirt, wearing a hat that read, "I'm having a bad hair day." We both smiled.

"Hello, sister," I said.

"Hello, sister," she replied.

She raised her hand and removed her hat. My sister had shaved her head. We stood there crying and laughing and hugging.

"We still look like sisters," was all she said.

"I love you," was all that I could say.

I shut my eyes and said a silent prayer, *Thank You, God, for my life. Thank You, God in heaven, for my sister.*[8]

I have many friends,

but only one sister.

JOANNA V. ROBERTS

Thank you for being my caring sister. When I needed a shoulder to cry on, you were always there. When no one seemed to understand me—you did. And when my world seemed to be falling apart at the seams, you were faithful to remind me that God would put it back together again.

VALENCIA SMITH

Sisterhood is the journey of celebrating life together.

KELLY KLINK

✺ ✺ ✺ ✺ ✺

Lord,

Through all of life's changing seasons—good and bad—my sister has been by my side with a helping hand, a shoulder to cry on, a warm embrace, or a contagious smile. She is my confidante, my wise counselor, and my closest friend.

My sister shares everything with me, and I know her very well. You, however, know her even better than I do. You know the desires of her heart, her deepest, secret longings. Father, I ask that You would fulfill those desires, pouring blessings into her life as she blesses those around her with her many talents and her joyful disposition.

When she is traveling through a valley in her life, help me to be sensitive to her needs and to be a source of comfort and strength for her. When she is celebrating a new opportunity, I want to be there to join in her jubilation.

Thank You for my precious sister who has blessed my life in so many ways.

Amen.

I THANK GOD for you,

my LOYAL sister!

You're the

BEST

SISTER

in the World Because...

We Have Memories

That Will Last

a Lifetime.

A sister shares the memories of yesterday,

the joys of today,

and the hopes of tomorrow.

AUTHOR UNKNOWN

The memory of the righteous will be a blessing.

PROVERBS 10:7

How long has it been since you've taken a stroll down memory lane with your sister? If it's been awhile, why not set aside some time today or in the near future for just such a stroll. Call her just to let her know you've been thinking about her and enjoy sharing a memory that comes to mind. Or set up a lunch date to reminisce. You could even visit a park or museum that was special to both of you when you were younger. Whatever you decide to do, your sister will appreciate the time you've set aside just for her, and you'll both reap the pleasure sharing precious memories brings.

As you reminisce over old times, include God in your conversation. Thank Him together for the blessing of sisterhood and for filling your past with sweet memories that have drawn you closer to one another. Express your gratitude for the gift of remembering and all the joy it brings.

A TRIBUTE TO MY SISTER

My sister is about seven years my senior, but when we were young, she would still play make-believe with me for hours on end. There was usually some compromise involved—I liked dolls and makeup, while she liked toy cars and building sets—but somehow we always made it work for both of us. Sometimes I was a princess, and she was in charge of all the knights who guarded my castle. Other times, my dolls would spend a day at the races watching her cars zip down the track.

We shared a room, and on weekend nights, my sister would sometimes let me sleep with her in the top bunk where we'd have our own little pajama party, inviting our favorite stuffed animals. Even though she was older and had friends and interests of her own, she always found time for me and helped create a wealth of memories that has bonded us together forever.

Thank You, Father, for my sister's vivid imagination and her willingness to not grow up too quickly. I'll always cherish those precious childhood memories.

KAELYN MORIAH

Some of the greatest gifts God has given are the special memories of a shared life together. Walking hand in hand through the rain. Dashing to see who could get to the ringing phone first. Eating ice cream from the same bowl. Fighting over who would wear that special blouse or those new jeans. Laughing over silly things that seemed only funny to us.

CAROLYN B. GEORGE

It is as if it were yesterday that we
played dolls by our twin beds.
We laughed and cried through our
exciting teenage years.
We were each other's maid of honor
when we got married.
We held each other's babies with
tears in our eyes.
We have been through everything
together and it's still the same.
We are best friends—we are sisters.

AMY S. BARTLETT

Pleasure is the flower

that passes; remembrance,

the lasting perfume.

JEAN DE BOUFFLERS

Sweet is the voice of a sister

in the season of sorrow.

BENJAMIN DISRAELI

I HAD FORGOTTEN

By Nancy Swiatek Pardo

Our real possession is our memory.
In nothing else are we rich, in nothing else are we poor.

ALEXANDER SMITTY

I had forgotten that I'd once been a princess. My sister reminded me.

We were doing something that I'd heard people do and always wondered how a person could bear to do it—go through their mother's things. My three sisters and I were in my mother's cramped apartment, trying to get as much done as possible before one sister and I returned to our out-of-town homes and families, leaving whatever work remained to the other two sisters. We wanted to get as much done together as we could and share the burden as well as the grief.

We did better at the former than the latter. My sisters epitomize the "when the going gets tough, the tough get going." We worked well together, but we mostly kept our grief to ourselves.

We didn't fight about who wanted what. If two sisters wanted something, they tried to gauge who it meant the most to and that's the sister who kept it. None of it was monetarily valuable; it was all about whose memory was wrapped around it.

My mom had the same jewelry box my whole life. It was jammed with all kinds of costume jewelry, from current things back to 1940s-era items. We packaged up most of it for the give-away pile.

I pulled out a bracelet. It is one of those kinds that expands to fit over the hand and then is snug about the wrist, like a watchband. It has three rows of faceted glass set in what looks like nickel plate.

"Anybody want this?" I asked, hoping, though I didn't know why, that they would all say no. I couldn't place the memory, but my gut told me there was something special connected with it.

Lorraine's face lit up. "Oh!" she said, "Do you remember this?"

"I do kind of, but I don't know why," I replied.

She took it out of my hand and placed it, open side down, on top of my head. Instantly, the memory came flooding back. When I was little, Lorraine, being ten years older, would take pity on the little sister and play with me. In the attic were crinolines from fashions gone by. She would dress me in the crinolines, drape my head in colorful scarves, and anchor them with the bracelet, its sparkling glass looking like the perfect tiara. A bobby pin here and there, a little lipstick and rouge, and *voila!* Instant princess!

All that flashed by in a moment as I looked at my dear sister, and all at once I was that little girl again, safe and treasured and loved in our cozy childhood home. Both of us blinked away tears as she wrapped me in a tight hug.

Our world would never be quite the same again. Standing on either side of our mother's bed as she died would change us somehow inexplicably forever. But we would still face that world together, our love for one another even surer.

Now when I wear the bracelet for a special occasion, inevitably someone will comment on how lovely it is. "It was my mother's," I say.

And I smile.[9]

Memories shared with a sister
are forever treasured.

AUTHOR UNKNOWN

✦ ✦ ✦ ✦ ✦

Heavenly Father,

Thank You for the immense joy having a sister has brought to my life. Because of her, I've always had someone to share my heart with, to play with, even to argue and make up with. When I look back on my childhood, I can't imagine what it would have been like had my sister not played such a principal part in it. The memories we've shared are among my most prized possessions in life.

As we continue to build on the memories that compose our sisterhood, may the bond we share only grow stronger with time. I pray we will never forget how to have fun together, how to be completely open in each other's presence, and how to offer forgiveness quickly and willingly when necessary.

Thank You for the privilege of being a part of each new phase in her life and for the honor of being called her sister.

Amen.

I THANK GOD for you,

my sister for a LIFETIME!

Sisters are for sharing—fun and laughter,

Arguments and fights,

Secrets and stories,

Makeup and purses,

Hard times and sadness,

Love and togetherness.

Sisters are for sharing—memories.

PRISCILLA COTTON

Who can explain or understand the bond between
two sisters? It is a gift beyond explanation.
It is a knowing, a trust, a love that captures all that is
good in life and displays it for all to see.
It is a relationship like no other.
The one who does not have it cannot imagine
what it would be like to have a sister.

R. M. KITE

NOTES

1 Paula Miller, Olivia, Minnesota. Story used by permission of author.
2 Andrea D'Asaro, Elkins Park, Pennsylvania. Story used by permission of author.
3 Gail E. Strock, Belleville, Pennsylvania. Story used by permission of author.
4 Sally Friedman, Moorestown, New Jersey. Story used by permission of author.
5 Carol Sterner, Tulsa, Oklahoma. Story used by permission of author.
6 Carol McAdoo Rehme, Loveland, Colorado. Story used by permission of author.
7 Deborah Hedstrom-Page, Springfield, Oregon. Story used by permission of author.
8 Dawn Braulick, Billings, Montana. Story used by permission of author.
9 Nancy Swiatek Pardo, Mount Prospect, Illinois. Story used by permission of author.

LOOK FOR THESE BOOKS:

THE BEST FRIEND
IN THE WORLD

THE BEST GRANDMA
IN THE WORLD

THE BEST TEACHER
IN THE WORLD

HOWARD BOOKS
A DIVISION OF SIMON & SCHUSTER
New York   London   Toronto   Sydney